HISTORY JOURNEYS

An Evacuee's Journey

Peter Hepplewhite

HODDER
Wayland

an imprint of Hodder Children's Books

Produced for Hodder Wayland by
Discovery Books Ltd
Unit 3, 37 Watling Street, Leintwardine, Shropshire SY7 0LW, England

First published in 2003 by Hodder Wayland, an imprint of
Hodder Children's Books

British Library Cataloguing in Publication Data
Hepplewhite, Peter
An evacuee's journey. - (History journeys)
1. Transportation - Great Britain - History - 20th century - Juvenile literature
2. World War, 1939-1945 - Evacuation of civilians - Great Britain - Juvenile
literature 3. Great Britain - History - George VI, 1936-1952 - Juvenile literature
I. Title
388' .0941'09044

0 7502 3957 3

Printed and bound by G. Canale & C. S.p.A. Italy

Designer: Ian Winton
Editor: Rebecca Hunter
Illustrations: Mark Bergin

Hodder Children's Books would like to thank the following
for the loan of their material:

Discovery Picture Library: page 6 (inset); **Hulton Archive:** *cover,* pages 4, 6, 8, 9,
11 (both), 12, 13 (both), 15, 16, 17, 20, 21, 23 (top), 24, 25, 27 (both), 28, 29; **Robert
Opie:** pages 7, 14, 18, 19 (both), 22, 23: **The Sunderland News:** page 26.
Sunderland Museum and Winter Gardens, Tyne and Wear Museums: page 5.

Hodder Children's Books
A division of Hodder Headline Limited
338 Euston Road
London NW1 3BH

CONTENTS

IF THE BOMBS START FALLING...

Joseph Thompson lived in Sunderland, near the River Wear. It was August 1939 and his dad was worried. 'I think there's going to be a war Joe,' he said. 'When the fighting starts I reckon the Germans will try to bomb the docks and the shipyards. You might have to go and live in the country for a while, where you'll be safe.'

In 1918 Germany had been defeated in the First World War. The German people felt humiliated and in 1933 they voted a strong leader into power - Adolf Hitler. Soon he was threatening the rest of Europe.

In March 1938 Germany took over Austria and six months later Hitler demanded control of the Sudetenland in Czechoslovakia. The British Prime Minister, Neville Chamberlain, flew to meet him at Munich and agreed to his claim. An uneasy calm lasted until March 1939 when German troops marched into the rest of Czechoslovakia. Now most British people realised that the only way to stop Hitler was by force.

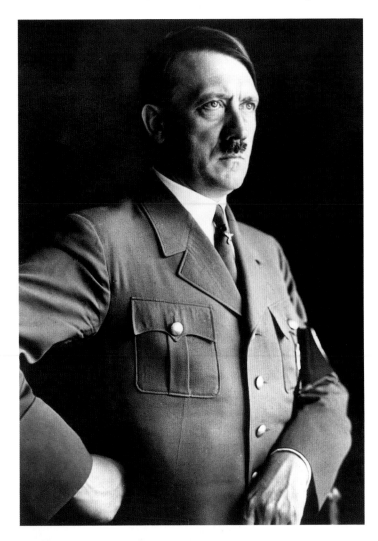

A portrait of Adolf Hitler, the German leader in 1939.

4

In 1939 Sunderland was known as 'the largest ship-building town in the world'. As Joe's dad feared, the shipyards became targets for German bombers in 1940.

Yet the thought of war was terrifying! Experts believed whole cities would be pounded into rubble by bombers. The British government began to prepare for the worst. In 1938 plans were made to save as many people as possible by getting them out of harm's way as soon as the fighting began. This was called evacuation.

Fearing the Worst

'London will be one vast madhouse, the hospitals will be attacked, traffic will stop, the homeless will shriek for help, the city will be a pandemonium.'

MAJOR-GENERAL J.F.C. FULLER 1938

● In March 1938 Italian bombers attacked Barcelona in Spain and killed 1,300 people. Gloomy British planners calculated that 72 people died for every tonne of bombs dropped. Using these figures - and what they guessed about the size of the German air force - they told the government to expect 150,000 dead and injured in the first few days of war.

● Luckily for Britain the experts were wrong! The German air force was not as powerful as they predicted. Sixty thousand British civilians died in air raids during the whole war. This was bad, but far less than expected.

PREPARING FOR WAR

It was 3 September 1939 and Joe was playing noisily with his toy Spitfire. 'Shhh,' said Dad sharply. 'The Prime Minister is on the radio.' Joe listened tight-lipped. 'I have to tell you that this country is now at war with Germany,' said the Prime Minister. 'Oh no,' thought Joe. 'It looks as if I will be sent away.'

Young children practice wearing their gas masks. Gas masks had to be carried at all times, but most children hated the smell of rubber and disliked wearing them.

Across the country children like Joe had become used to the idea of war. In 1938 almost 40 million gas masks had been issued in case the Germans dropped poisonous gas bombs. Schools held regular air-raid drills. Children put on their rubber masks and sat in the cellars, air-raid shelters or newly dug trenches.

(Below) Some children had 'Mickey Mouse' gas masks. They were supposed to be less frightening and more fun to wear.

This playing card shows the contrast between the dirty cities and the pleasant countryside of the reception areas.

For the evacuation scheme, the country was divided into three areas: evacuation, neutral and reception zones. The idea was to move millions of children, mothers and disabled people out of the cities (the evacuation zones) into the countryside (the reception zones). Those who stayed behind would keep essential industries and services running, like munitions works, transport and hospitals. The neutral zones were lower risk areas where people were not disturbed.

Parents are reminded that the children must take with them:—

An overcoat or mackintosh, and the following suggested changes of clothing:—

Girls:— One vest or combinations, one pair of knickers, one bodice, one petticoat, two pairs of stockings, handkerchiefs, gym slip and blouse, hat, cardigan.

Boys:— One vest, one shirt with collar, one pair of underpants, one jersey or pullover, one pair of trousers, handkerchiefs, two pairs of socks or stockings, cap.

In addition, they all must carry night-clothes, comb and brush, slippers or sand shoes, towel, soap, facecloth, tooth brush, and if possible an extra pair of boots or shoes.

No one was forced to be evacuated, but mothers were firmly told they would be putting their children in danger if they did not send them away. Families could make their own arrangements - with friends or relatives - or they could take part in the plans made by their local councils.

This article from the *Sunderland Echo* 6 September 1939, tells children what clothes to take with them during evacuation.

EVACUATION!

Joe was evacuated with his school. He kissed his parents goodbye at the school gates, and tried not to cry. The children walked in a crocodile to nearby Millfield Station, led by their teachers. They were going by train to East Yorkshire. Joe was frightened and excited at the same time - at 10 years old, he had never been on a train or even left Sunderland before.

During the first days of September 1939, one and a half million people took part in the official evacuation and around two million made their own way to safer areas. Many children, like Joe, were evacuated in school parties and said goodbye to their parents in the playground.

A group of London schoolchildren waving goodbye to their families as they leave for Blackhorse Road Station.

Most evacuees left by train, travelling to stations by tram, bus or on foot. Like an army on the move they carried their equipment - gas masks, lunches, suitcases or backpacks of clothes and perhaps a favourite toy. Attached to them were labels with their name, school number and destination - in case anyone got lost on the busy platforms.

Sunderland Education Committee

FIRST DAY
Evacuation of School Children on SUNDAY, 10th September, 1939

All School Children who wish to be Evacuated Must Assemble AT SCHOOL at the time shown below:—

Entraining at MONKWEARMOUTH STATION

School.	Time of Assembly at School a.m.
St. Mary's R.C.	7.00
St. Benet's R.C.	7.00
Moor	7.00
Hudson Road	7.00
Redby	7.15
Fulwell	7.15
Stansfield Street	8.30
Monkwearmouth C.E.	8.30
Monkwearmouth Central	9.00
St. Columba's C.E.	10.30
Grange Park	10.30

Nursery School Assemble at Station at 9.15

Entraining at MILLFIELD STATION

School.	Time of Assembly at School a.m.
Hendon	7.00
West Park	7.30
Junior Technical	7.30
Valley Road	7.30
Bede Girls	8.30
Bishopwearmouth C.E.	8.45
High Southwick	9.00
West Southwick	9.00
(Continued in Next Column)

(Continued from Previous Column)

	a.m.
Bede Boys	9.30
Chester Road	10.00
Thomas Street	10.00
Commercial Road	11.30
Garden Street	11.45

Entraining at PALLION STATION

School.	Time of Assembly at School a.m.
Diamond Hall	7.00
Hylton Road	8.00
Cowan Terrace	8.00
Green Terrace	8.00
St. Andrew's C.E.	9.30
Deptford Terrace	9.30
Simpson Street	9.30
St. Patrick's R.C.	9.30
Pallion	9.45
St. Hilda's R.C.	10.00
St. Joseph's R.C.	10.45
James Williams Street	10.45
	p.m.
Barnes	12.30
St. John's C.E.	12.30
St. Paul's C.E.	12.30

To Travel by Bus

	a.m.
Fordhall	9.00

W. THOMPSON,
Director of Education and Evacuation Officer.

'Most of the children had risen early and after standing in queues for the trains with heavy packs on their backs, were tired. One little girl clutched a huge dolly in her arms.

A 14 year-old boy played a mouth organ and encouraged his companions to sing.'

SUNDERLAND ECHO 11 SEPTEMBER 1939

Most towns began their evacuation schemes on 1 September 1939, two days before the war began. However Sunderland was designated a neutral area and it was not until war broke out that this was changed. The Sunderland evacuation did not begin until 10 September, as this article from the *Sunderland Echo* shows.

The evacuation was the biggest movement of people in British history. And London was especially busy. On 1 September a packed train left each of the main stations every nine minutes. In three days 660,000 evacuees were moved out - 377,000 children looked after by their teachers, 275,000 mothers and children travelling together, 3,500 pregnant women and a similar number of blind adults.

- Some parents refused to part with their children - in spite of the warnings. 'If we are going to die, we'll die together,' some said.

- Only 50 percent of London children were evacuated, around 40 percent in Glasgow, 30 percent in Sunderland and only 15 percent in Sheffield.

THE RAILWAY JOURNEY

The train chugged slowly out of the station, every window jammed with boys and girls laughing and giving the thumbs up sign. The journey took a long time and Joe was glad his mother had made sandwiches. He shared them with friends who had not brought anything to eat. It was late afternoon when the train pulled into Driffield and everyone was tired.

In the 1930s most people going on a long journey took the train. In Britain, even tiny villages were usually only a few kilometres from a station. This meant that while a number of young evacuees left by bus or even by boat, most left by railway.

This map shows the route of Joe's journey from Sunderland to Middleton-on-the-Wolds in the Yorkshire countryside.

For some the journey was like a holiday. Many poor children saw the countryside for the first time from the train window and marvelled at the green, open spaces. They chatted excitedly, shared sandwiches and sang. High spirits led to high jinks. Norah Hodgkin, travelling from Suffolk to Gloucestershire, vividly recalled travelling through the long Ipswich tunnel, and frightening the teachers in the dark!

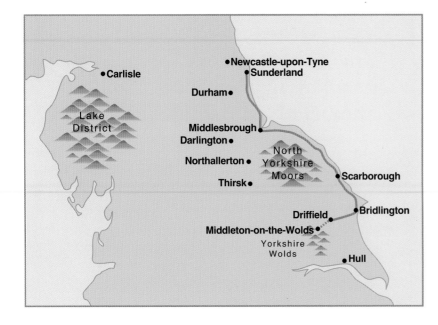

A packed evacuation train ready to leave.

For others it was a miserable day. Evacuee trains were slotted in between regular services and spent hours covering short distances. Unlucky children travelled in carriages without corridors and toilets and many little ones were sick or soiled their pants. Often they did not arrive at their destinations until late at night - exhausted, dirty and hungry.

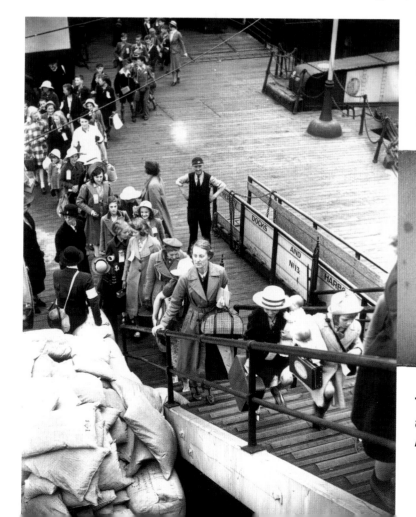

'A lady in a green uniform leaned in the train window and gave us all a little packet of nuts and raisins and an orange. I poked my finger into the orange and sucked out all the juice and discarded the rest. I didn't see another orange until after the war.'

EVACUEE JOYCE FRY

Thousands of evacuees were sent abroad by ship to the USA, Canada, Australia and New Zealand.

FOSTER FAMILIES

J oe and his class were put on buses to take them to nearby villages. They soon arrived at Middleton-on-the-Wolds. After a short wait in the school hall, local families arrived to look at the evacuees - and pick one or two to take home with them. Joe was one of the last to be chosen. He was feeling very miserable, when a big, smiling woman said to him 'You look ready for a good meal my lad. You'd better come with me.'

This group of evacuees from London are waiting in a village hall for their new homes to be allocated.

The reception areas had been preparing for the evacuation for weeks. Billeting officers were the officials in charge of finding accommodation for evacuees. They collected lists of families who had volunteered to act as foster parents to city children - or to take in an adult. If there were not enough volunteers, the officers could order people to take in evacuees. If they refused they could be fined money. Not surprisingly this caused a lot of anger.

Evacuees arriving by bus in a country village.

The evacuees or 'vacs', were selected for billeting in two ways. Some, like Joe, gathered in school or church halls and were chosen by their hosts. Others were taken in small groups from house to house and either accepted or turned away at the front door.

● A foster parent was paid 10 shillings (s) and 6 pence (d) billeting allowance to look after a single child or 8s 6d per child where there were two or more. This was to cover food and lodgings. Clothes were to be paid for by parents. To the annoyance of many foster parents they received the same whether they were looking after a 5 year-old or a teenager.

● Although these allowances sound small, the average weekly wage for a man in 1938 was £2 13s 3d a week, so 10s 6d was more than a quarter of the weekly income of many families.

A smiling foster mother shakes hands with children who will be staying in her home.

A NATIONAL DISGRACE

Joe found he was to be billeted with Mrs Richardson, a farmer's wife. She fed him a grand meal, ran him a hot bath and put him to bed. But Joe felt uncomfortable when she unpacked his haversack. He knew that his clothes were old and worn-out. His father had been unemployed for four years and his mother had struggled to make do with the 'dole' money.

During the 1930s a lot of people were out of work in Britain; as many as 3 million by 1933. Around one third of families had to live on unemployment payments from the government, usually called 'the dole'. Dole payments were small - about 30 shillings a week for a family of four.

Much of the money went on rent, leaving too little for nourishing food or new clothes. Yet people in the wealthier areas of the country knew little of the problem. The poor were out of sight in the slum areas of the towns and cities - until evacuation thrust their children in front of a shocked country.

Young evacuees line up for their daily dose of cod liver oil.

Foster parents were often horrified at the state of the young evacuees they had taken in. They were often dirty and many arrived with only the clothes they stood in. The poorest had no socks and no knickers.

'One boy said he never went to sleep lying down. He perched himself by the bedpost and went to bed with his head resting on it. There had never been room in an overcrowded bed for him to lie down.'

A REPORT FROM A HEADMISTRESS IN CHEPSTOW, 1939

• One nickname for evacuees in Wales was 'skinnies' because they looked so thin compared to country children.

• The condition of the evacuees helped to persuade politicians that something had to be done to end poverty. After the war the Labour government set up the Welfare State to look after people 'from the cradle to the grave'.

Thousands were badly nourished, infested with lice and carried infectious diseases such as scabies and impetigo. The government acted quickly to improve their health, paying for free milk in schools and cod liver oil for children under five.

THE LUCKY ONES

J oe soon settled in with his foster family. Mrs Richardson didn't have any children and enjoyed having him to look after and feed. Mr Richardson showed him round the farmyard and Joe loved meeting the farm animals and making friends with the sheepdogs. His first letter home began 'Dear Mam and Dad. Having a smashing time...' And he meant it!

These lucky evacuees are moving into an old country house near Cheltenham.

To comfort worried parents, newspapers were full of articles about evacuees enjoying themselves. The *Sunderland Echo* was typical. A reporter visited the villages around Driffield and wrote: 'For the children this last week has been a glorious holiday. Among the happiest are 18 living in Middleton Hall, a huge mansion with hundreds of acres of parkland. "We have two helpers, three servants and a cook to look after us," said 13 year-old Iris Forbisher.'

After a day's work helping on the fields in Devon, these lads feel they have earned a ride home in the farmer's wheelbarrow.

And whether they were billeted in a mansion or humble cottage, it was true that many evacuees had the time of their lives. They had caring foster parents and came to love country life: the fresh air, farm animals, exercise and healthy food. And many settled in contentedly, helping in pheasant shoots, snaring rabbits or bringing in the harvest. They grew up quickly and learned to cope with new situations by themselves.

'The people in the villages to which we were sent are homely people like ourselves, none of them are well off but none are hard up. They all grow their own food and there will be no shortages here.' Mrs Thacker, reported in the *Sunderland Echo*, 20 September 1939.

NOT SO LUCKY

Joe's best friend, Tom Henderson, was billeted with a gamekeeper and his family. One day he showed Joe some bruises on his back. 'He doesn't really want me in his house and he hits me for the smallest thing I do wrong.' After a few weeks of this treatment, Tom wrote to his mother and she came and took him back to Sunderland.

This sentimental song written for evacuees was a big hit with parents and children alike.

Although the newspapers wrote few stories about it, lots of evacuees had a dismal time. Homesickness and bedwetting were common. The famous actor Michael Caine was evacuated from the East End of London with his brother. He remembered: 'Clarence and I used to sleep together and poor Clarence used to wet the bed, 'cause he was a very nervous kid. She [his foster mother, a policeman's wife] could never tell who done it so she used to bash the daylights out of both of us.'

'We were re-housed to a young mother no more than 19, whose husband was in the army. The house was in a very poor state; orange boxes for a cupboard. She was hardly able to look after herself and her baby.'

CHRISTINE PRING, AGED 12 IN 1939

Problem Billets

'There wasn't much physical cruelty, mainly mental. She [foster mother] would say to us 'Don't tell anyone your parents live in a flat, only people who have done wrong live in flats.' She used to sell our sweet coupons every time they were issued...'

MARJORIE, AGED 6 IN 1939

This government poster set out to persuade mothers to keep their children in the country.

Some hosts resented the children who were 'dumped on them' while others were too old, sick or busy to take care of fretful evacuees. No attempt was made to match children to foster parents with similar backgrounds. A child from a Glasgow slum could end up with a professional family with posh English accents. At worst, hosts and evacuees couldn't even understand each other. Children who were sent to North Wales sometimes found themselves billeted with Welsh speakers and had to learn a totally new language.

These characters are from a card game based on the evacuation. The game tried to make being an evacuee look fun.

19

BACK TO SCHOOL

One week after he had settled in at the Richardson's, Joe's teachers came round with some news. School was about to start! The teachers had decided to start lessons for the evacuees in the village hall. Joe's days exploring the farm were about to end, but he had always enjoyed school and looked forward to meeting up with some other children.

An unusual 'school bus' carries children from the widely scattered farms where they are billeted.

Teachers were a vital part of the evacuation scheme. They visited children in their billets, handled complaints, wrote to parents and filled in endless forms for milk, visits to the clinic and clothing. But what better way to make life as normal as possible for their pupils than get them back to school?

There were problems at first when the local children and evacuees first met up. Fighting and name-calling often followed. The solution to this was often split-shift teaching - half a day for local children and half a day for evacuees - became common.

These evacuees are being taught about the months of the year in an emergency school in the Church of St Mary the Virgin, Little Ilford, Essex.

A shortage of buildings for lessons was another problem. However, keen teachers rose to the challenge. While the summer weather lasted they organized nature rambles to collect wild flowers or visits to farms to watch the cows being milked and animals being fed. Later, arrangements were made to share local schools or church halls. Because equipment of all kinds was in short supply, many lessons became more practical with children taking part in plays, concerts and debates.

Making do

Conditions in emergency buildings could be hard. Teacher Margaret Woodrow recalled: 'There was no room at the local school and my classroom was in the village hall, a wood and corrugated iron building with a heater that smoked. At first we had to manage with just rough books and pencils. The sole lavatory was a bench seat with a hole in it and a bucket underneath, in a shed like a sentry box. A senior pupil would stand guard while the teacher used it.'

Parents worried that their children's education was suffering but the government didn't think so. The chief inspector for schools wrote that spelling and maths might have fallen behind a little but 'there can be no doubt that many children's lives have been greatly enriched... by first hand experience.'

SHORTAGES AND RATIONING

When he wasn't at school, Joe loved helping on the farm. As the weeks went by he learned to feed the pigs and chickens but Mr Richardson warned him not to treat them like pets. 'Don't get too fond of them Joe.' he said. 'One day we will have to sell them at the market. We are at war now and Britain needs all the food it can get.'

To keep on fighting, Britain needed to import a vast range of supplies, everything from potatoes to petrol. As soon as the war began, German submarines, called U-boats, started to sink British ships. The German navy knew that if they could sink enough, Britain would grind to a halt and her people would starve.

This was the week's rations for one person in 1943.

To share food fairly, rationing began in January 1940, starting with sugar, butter and bacon. Everyone was given a ration book. It held coupons that were taken out when goods were bought. By 1943 weekly rations per person were: butter 2 ^{1}/$_2$oz (57g), margarine 4oz (104g), cooking fat 2 ^{1}/$_2$oz (57g), sugar 8oz (226g), tea 2 ^{1}/$_2$oz (57g), cheese 1oz (28g) and jam 1lb (450g), a month. Meat was rationed by price at 1s 2d worth a week.

Two boys feeding chickens on a small farm run by evacuees at Epworth near Doncaster.

British farmers and gardeners had to produce as much food as possible. An extra 2.5 million hectares of land was ploughed up and even the flower-beds of Buckingham Palace became vegetable plots. Lots of evacuees, like Joe, helped out on farms, especially at harvest time.

For a healthy, happy job

Join the **WOMEN'S LAND ARMY**

APPLY TO NEAREST W.L.A. COUNTY OFFICE OR TO W.L.A. HEADQUARTERS 6 CHESHAM PLACE LONDON S.W.1

● In the first months of the war U-boats sank around 100,000 tonnes of ships a month. But in the last seven months of 1940 this figure soared to 250,000 tonnes. U-boat captains called this 'the happy time' - they were winning!

● Bread and potatoes - 'filler foods' - were never rationed. Foods that were expensive to import such as bananas, tinned fruit and grapes disappeared altogether.

Land girls helped to keep the farms running while the men were away fighting.

23

THE BATTLE OF BRITAIN

The weeks soon turned into months for the evacuees - and with the new year came new worries. In July 1940 Joe heard on the radio that Britain was threatened with invasion. Over the next three months battles raged in the skies as German bombers attacked British cities. On 14 August Joe watched as 150 German fighters and bombers from Norway attacked the cities in northern England.

1940 was a bad year for Britain and her allies, as defeat followed defeat. In April the Germans conquered Denmark and Norway and in May struck at France with an attack through the Netherlands and Belgium. The French, and the British army which had gone to help them, collapsed in the face of this German blitzkreig, or 'lightning war'.

In June the British army staged a desperate escape from the beaches of Dunkirk. The Royal Navy rescued the men but they had to leave their equipment - tanks, artillery and even rifles behind. For a few months Britain was weak and vulnerable to invasion. The Local Defence Volunteers or Home Guard was called up to stop spies, saboteurs and paratroopers preparing the way for the German army.

A unit of Home Guards and cadets (young soldiers) under inspection.

A Hurricane and Spitfire in flight – the planes that saved Britain during the Battle of Britain.

Luckily the Royal Air Force (RAF) Fighter Command was ready and waiting. Top-secret radar sets detected German aircraft soon after they took off and fast Hurricanes and Spitfire fighters were sent to intercept them by highly organized control rooms. After three months of fierce fighting the German air force, the Luftwaffe, was unable to gain air superiority over British skies. In September Hitler cancelled his plan to invade Britain.

● 3,080 pilots fought for Fighter Command during the Battle of Britain and 515 of them were killed.

● The RAF destroyed 1,733 Luftwaffe planes and lost 915 of their own.

25

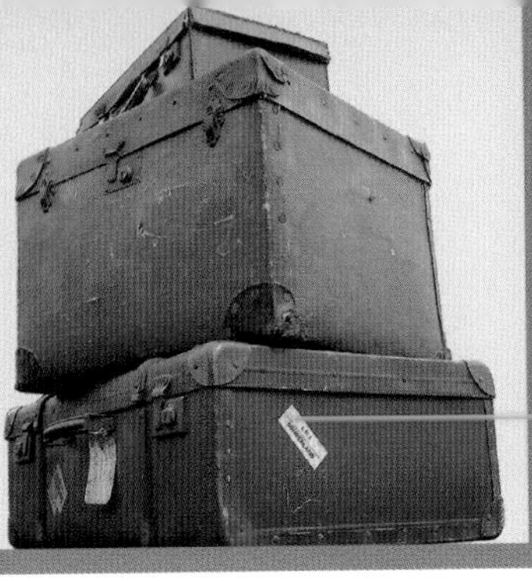

THE BLITZ

The German Air Force have used this map of the Sunderland Dock Area to plan their bombing raids. They have marked up the areas that they wish to target.

By September 1940 Joe had been away for almost a year. Many Sunderland children had been brought home and Joe's parents were thinking of sending for him when the Blitz began. As bombs fell on Sunderland his mother wrote: 'I miss you very much but it's not safe to come home now. The Germans have even bombed the toy shop.'

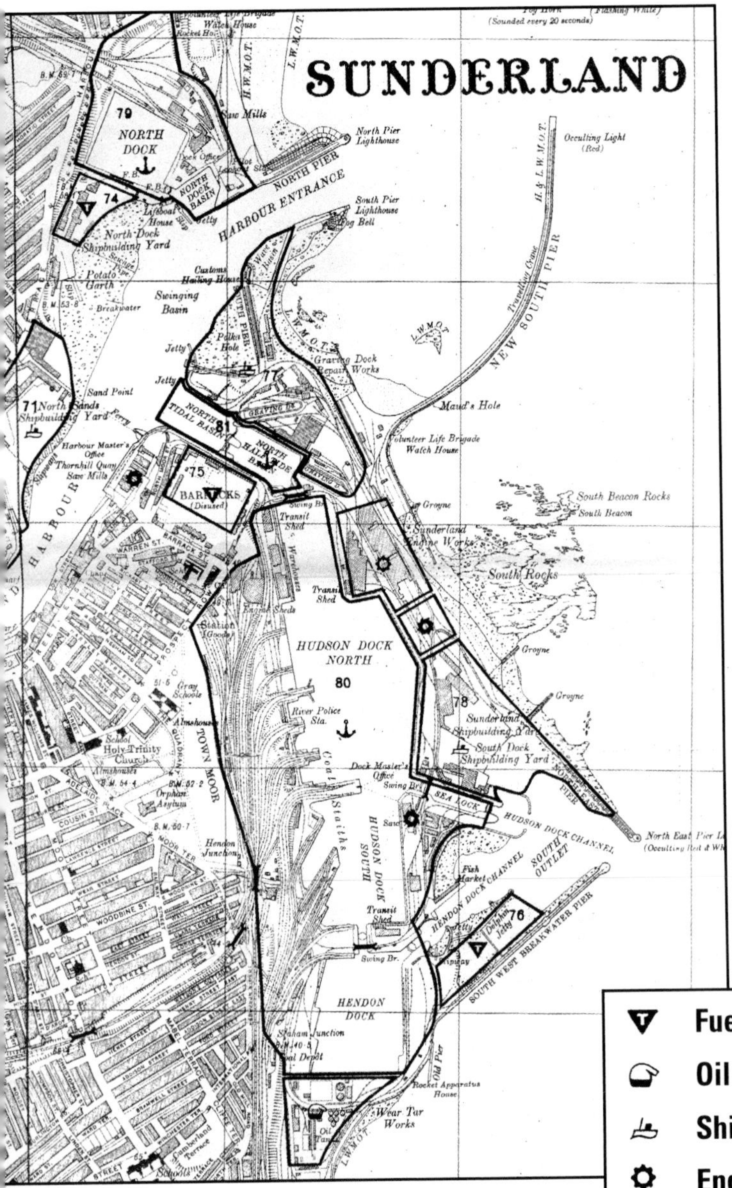

In the eyes of the government, evacuation had not been a success. Too many parents had not sent their children to safety in the first place - or had brought them home early. There were several reasons for this. Some families were too poor. They lived on the dole and received money for each child at home. They could not afford the cut in benefits if the children went away. Others missed their children so much they couldn't bear to be without them. Most had thought evacuation was a waste of time during the so-called 'Phoney War' - the quiet months after September 1939 when nothing seemed to be happening.

Fuel storage	Docks
Oil Tanks	Saw Mill
Ship building dock	Railway bridge
Engineering Works	Road bridge

'When the all-clear goes there is a groan of relief. But as soon as people get outside the shelter, there are screams of horror at the sight of the damage...smashed windows and roofs everywhere...smoke streaming across the sky from the docks.'

LONDON 8 SEPTEMBER, 1940

London Docks ablaze during the first mass air raid on London on 7 September 1940.

This feeling changed suddenly in September 1940 when the Germans bombed London and other cities. The Blitz had begun. During the autumn of 1940 over a million mothers and children took part in a second evacuation. And not a moment too soon as casualties grew. The first heavy raid on London on 7 September killed 306 people and injured 1,337. And that was only the beginning. Air raids lasted until 10 May 1941 and almost 20,000 Londoners died.

A bombed street in Coventry during the Blitz.

● A 'Blitz' was a heavy air raid in which more than 100 German bombers attacked a city on one night.

● On 14 November 1940 the German air force bombed Coventry. In one of the worst raids of the war 554 people were killed.

THE THIRD GREAT EVACUATION

Joe's evacuation went on for four long years. The last air raids on Sunderland took place in May 1943. As the quiet nights stretched on through the summer his parents decided to risk bringing him home. He was 14 when he left the Richardsons - glad to be going home but heartbroken to be leaving Middleton. He never forgot his new 'family' and visited the Richardsons every summer for many years after the war finished.

An artist paints amidst the ruins. Miraculously St Paul's Cathedral survived almost undamaged by German attacks on London.

By the spring of 1944, the German air force was too weak to make more than occasional attacks on British towns. Thousands of evacuees took the chance to return home, but for those living in the South of England the Germans had a nasty shock in store. In June 1944 the first V1 bombs fell on London. These flying bombs were also known as doodlebugs, because of the droning noise they made. When the noise stopped, you knew they were going to fall. By August almost 1. 5 million people had fled the capital - and several hundred of them were evacuated to Sunderland.

In those towns safe from flying bombs the end of the evacuation scheme - 'de-vacuation' began on 6 December 1944. In the South of England the trains began to roll home in March 1945.

But returning was tough for lots of evacuees. Like Joe, they had been away during the years when they changed from children into teenagers. Emotions were mixed. Some missed their foster parents deeply. They didn't recognize their mothers and fathers at first and it took them months to fit back into their families. Others couldn't wait to get home. Evacuation had been a wartime duty they had put up with and the sooner it was over the better.

For many children who lived through the war, being an evacuee was a happy experience that they would never forget.

TIMELINE

1918 — The end of the First World War.

1933 — Adolf Hitler becomes leader of Germany.

1938 — German troops occupy the Sudetenland in Czechoslovakia.

1939 — March: German troops march into the rest of Czechoslovakia.
1 September: Evacuation Scheme begins in British cities.
3 September: Germany invades Poland, Britain and France declare war on Germany.
10 September: The Sunderland Evacuation begins.
Christmas: Over half the total number of evacuees now back home.

1940 — January: Food rationing begins.
April: Germany conquers Denmark and Norway.
May: The fall of France.
The Home Guard is set up to protect Britain from German invasion
June: British troops are rescued from the beaches of Dunkirk by the Royal Navy.
The Battle of Britain begins.
September: The Blitz, attacks by bombers on British cities, begins. This leads to the second great evacuation.
November: Air raid on Coventry kills over 500 people.

1941 — May: The end of the London Blitz.
December: Japan attacks the USA and Great Britain.

1944 — June: Doodlebug attacks on London and the South East cause the third large wave of evacuations.

1945 — May: The end of the war in Europe.
August: Japan surrenders after atomic bombs are dropped on Hiroshima and Nagasaki.

GLOSSARY

air-raid siren — A loud noise to warn of an approaching attack by enemy bombers.

allies — Britain, the USA and the USSR fought together as allies against Germany, Italy and Japan during the war.

billeting officers — Officials in charge of finding accommodation for the evacuees.

Blitzkreig — A German word meaning 'Lightning War'; the use of aircraft, tanks and artillery moving so quickly that nothing could stop them.

dole — Benefit paid by the state to the unemployed.

doodlebugs — The German V1 bomb, named because of the noise it made.

evacuation zone — Places most likely to be bombed.

foster parents — People who had young evacuees to stay in their homes.

gamekeeper — A worker who breeds, tends and protects animals to be hunted.

gas masks — Masks that were worn over the face to protect people from poisonous gases that might be used during the war.

high jinks — fun

Home Guard — The volunteer force set up to defend Britain against invasion.

impetigo — An infectious rash on the face and body.

import — To bring in from abroad.

military exercise — War games to teach soldiers how to fight.

munitions works — Places where military weapons, ammunition and equipment were made.

neutral areas — Places unlikely to be bombed.

pandemonium — chaos

radar — Short for **RA**dio **D**etection **A**nd **R**anging

rationing — Government control of supplies, to ensure everyone got the same amount during times of shortage.

reception zones — Areas accepting those who had been evacuated.

saboteurs — Agents who might attack key targets like power stations or railway lines.

scabies — A disease that spreads easily and causes itchy skin.

shilling — An amount of money worth 12 old pence (5p in today's money).

Sudetenland — An area of Czechoslovakia where lots of Germans lived.

voluntary — Not forced on people.

FURTHER READING

The Children's War by Ruth Ingliss, Collins, 1989
Wish You Were Here by W. W. Lowther, Walton Publications, 1989
The Home Front by Stewart Ross, Hodder Wayland, 1990
Children of the Blitz by Robert Westall, Macmillan, 1999

INDEX